Orpheus, Turning

Faith Shearin

2016

Orpheus, Turning

Cover painting: Orpheus and Eurydice
Edward John Poynter (March 1836 – July 1919)

ISBN 978-1-940120-97-3
Library of Congress Control Number: 2015953556

The Broadkill River Press
Broadkill Publishing Associates, LLC
P.O. Box 63
Milton, Delaware
www.thebroadkillriverpress.com

Orpheus, Turning

Acknowledgments:

Several of the poems in this manuscript have appeared previously, sometimes in slightly different form:
"Music at My Mother's Funeral" in *Alaska Quarterly Review*,
"Orpheus, Turning", "The Children of Hamelin", and
"Amelia Earhart's First Flight" in *Comstock Review*,
"Chasing Fireflies" in *Cold Mountain Review*,
"The Dog Watched Television" in *The Sun*,
"The Land of Nod" in *Salamander*,
"Our House, Surrounded by Animals" in *Slipstream*, and
“Mailing Babies” in *The Burnside Review*.

Thanks to the Friday Writers: Melanie Sumner, Adrienne Su, Raymond Atkins, and Tamara Powell. And thanks to my family: my husband and daughter, my parents and grandmother, my sister and brother. Thanks, as always, to Jack Driscoll and Michael Delp who first gave me poetry.

"I don't know what it means and I don't care because it's Shakespeare and it's like having jewels in my mouth when I say the words."

-- Frank McCourt,
Angela's Ashes

"If I plant a honeycomb outside my house, then it will grow up into a beehive."

--A.A. Milne
The House At Pooh Corner

Dedication

For Tom and Mavis and Turtle and Rapunzel
and Wookiee and our life on North Mountain

Table of Contents

Directions to Childhood	9
Marie Curie	10
The Change	11
The Past Wants You Back	12
Aliens	13
Directions	14
Orpheus, Turning	15
Music at My Mother's Funeral	16
The Children of Hamelin	17
My Grandfather's Last Errand	18
The Dog Watched Television	19
Amelia Earhart's First Flight	20
Hamelin Without the Rats	21
The Silk Road	22
My Brother, Trying To Go Home	23
Orpheus Singing in the Underworld	24
Titanic Survivors Found On Board	25
At Twelve	26
Ferry Ride to Ocracoke	27
Sight	28
This Fawn In Our Meadow	29
The Dead Take Vacations	30
Possum in the Garbage	32
Algebra	33
Polio Summer	34
Winter Arrives	35
Astronauts	36
Directions To Your College Dorm	37
Quarantine, 1918	38
Fishing Pier	39
The Weather in Hamelin	40

Dunes, At Night 41
My Mother, Eating Chocolate 42
Desert 43
He Was About to Come Home 44
My Father, Eating 45
Tire Swing 46
Angry Fathers 47
Dog Guarding a House in Pompeii 49
Grendel's Mother 50
Chasing Fireflies 52
The Feejee Mermaid 53
The Owl 54
Bermuda Triangle 55
Early Hominids Slept in Trees 56
How Dinosaurs Died 57
Lover's Eyes 58
Missing My Grandfather 59
My Mother, Running Away From Home 60
Mailing Babies 61
Picking Apples With My Father 62
Visiting Emily's House 63
My Mother, Dreaming of Privacy 64
Weather 65
My Life in a Picasso Painting 66
Jellyfish 67
The Land of Nod 68
Our House, Surrounded by Animals 69
Addresses 70
Portsmouth Island 71
Meet Me In Hamelin 72

About the Author 73

Directions to Childhood

Find an old woman in a studio, painting;
notice her cats standing
in the avenues of the past with their tails

curved like question marks. Upstairs,
a record player is tracing some ancient music
and, down the hall, there is a mirror

that will watch your hair darken. Now,
the old woman sits with you at a piano
and her hands have become wings;

now, she has taken you fishing on a pier
and, beneath you, the ocean is also
a wolf. This is childhood: your short dog

still climbing the stairs, your failures
as gentle as shade. You will only
sleep here a few more years. The woodpile,

to your right, is filling with spiders.
The Greek family, next door, has a pride
of stone lions that are learning your name.

Marie Curie

In those days, her discoveries in the future, she was drawn
to the glowing rocks, placed them on her bedside table
like a candle. The things that would happen to her

were inside: elements, papers, the day her husband,
weak from radiation, was crushed by horses
while crossing the road. Her affair with Paul

could be isolated from her own growing exhaustion,
the x-ray van she drove through the war.
Her papers are so toxic no one touches them now

without wearing lead. Gone are the radium night lights,
the radium toothpastes, the clock faces made luminous
by a faint blue paint. Marie placed her rocks

on a table and they called to her the way
the horizon calls baby sea turtles to the sea.

The Change

I never liked bleeding

so I was surprised to miss my body's scripted
regularity, its ruined cradle. They called it

the change when I was a child,
my grandmothers whispering to one another

behind the hung laundry, in the yard,
where they scrubbed the absence of stains.

I knew they felt hot and sometimes angry,
their clothes and wedding rings tight

like something outgrown. My hormones
receded and I could see suddenly

what they saw: the exhausted
window fans, the empty bread pans,

all that coffee percolating on the stove.

The Past Wants You Back

The past wants you back. It wants you to leave
whatever you're doing now:
eating oysters, brushing your hair,

and return to the scenes where
you were already yourself.
The past wants you to step into

the picture frame, to be ignorant
and thin. It wants you to like
the boy who cheated on you,

to wear the unflattering dress;
it requires you to take piano lessons
and catch strep throat,

then Chicken Pox. The past needs you.
Every day someone dies
and, with them, all the scenes

from those rooms. Every day
another key is lost and another building
crumbles. The past demands that

you wear a hat, that you
eat your dead aunt's casserole.

Aliens

They are coming in their glowing discs with many windows,
with their huge bald heads shaped like lightbulbs;
they are coming at night, in deserts, on abandoned

back roads, in a streak of red that resembles
a sunset. They have been preparing to take over
our neighborhoods: examining our bodies,

wearing shimmering jumpsuits, reading our minds.
In their distant galaxy they are planning for expansion
and they have been noticing our canyons

and fast food restaurants, admiring our music
and high heeled shoes. Some say they were
here long ago, building Egyptian pyramids

and statues on Easter Island, exploring our oceans
and speaking with whales. We are afraid
of them; we are excited by them; we have been

anticipating their arrival. The aliens are coming
from a planet we cannot find with our telescopes
and they are smarter than we are but they don't have

velvet Elvis posters or plastic Halloween fangs.
We tell stories about them, give them credit
for ancient miracles, say they stole us

from our beds and we cannot explain the strange
marks on our necks, the lost hours, the circles
that appeared overnight, in our fields.

Directions

Turn left by the grove of trees which grow taller
in my dreams. Then, drive backwards twenty five years.
You'll pass the city of candles
and the city of clocks. You'll pass the people

who knew you once and the ones who know you still.
You may want to have dinner in the windy town
by the sea where you imagined a life
you did not live. You are close now and there

is a trail lit by the moon where your pebbles
still glow. You know how to follow what has fallen
and when you do this you will find us,
as we once were, on that blanket in the meadow

with our mason jars and philosophy books,
with your arm draped over my shoulders.
You will remember the exact flavor of that spring,
the cottage you showed me where

our words might have blossomed on vines.
I know there was no future for us but there
is still a past where it always late afternoon
and we have been walking together
and I wear your laughter like clothes.

Orpheus, Turning

You can see how it happened: he was worried
and he wanted to be certain. He stepped into
the light and turned, as he might have before

his young wife was bitten, to see her expression,
to be sure her footsteps were real. For days
he traveled through the dark tunnel

from the underworld, never peering
over his shoulder. Then, just as he might have
reclaimed happiness, he turned, unable

to resist any longer the urge to look, and this
is how he lost her again, for Eurydice
was still in the realm of the dead. He turned

too soon, was too eager, and I watch him there,
his grief returning to him instead of his wife:
his new companion.

Music at My Mother's Funeral

During the weeks when we all believed my mother
was likely to die she began to plan
her funeral and she wanted us, her children,
to consider the music we would play there. We remembered
the soundtrack of my mother's life: the years when she swept
the floors to the sound of an eight track cassette called Feelings,
the Christmas when she bought a Bing Crosby album
about a Bright Hawaiian Christmas Day. She got Stravinsky's
Rite of Spring stuck in the tape deck of her car and for months
each errand was accompanied by some kind
of dramatic movement. After my brother was born,
there was a period during which she wore a muumuu
and devoted herself to King Sunny Ade and his
African beats. She ironed and wept to Evita, painted
to Italian opera. Then, older and heavier, she refused
to fasten her seatbelt and there was the music
of an automated bell going off every few minutes,
which annoyed the rest of us but did not seem to matter
to my mother who ignored its relentless disapproval,
its insistence that someone was unsafe.

The Children of Hamelin

Who knows what they were thinking when they left
their beds, warm with firelight, abandoned
their bread and honey and cups of milk;

parents watched them walk out of fenced yards,
fly out of swings, drop toys so gently they might still
be falling. Only the rats understood how it felt

to be called from the places that were familiar
and safe; only they knew how the Piper's music
sounded when it was meant for you.

Lemmings sometimes hear it
and sea turtles, returning
to their homeland to lay eggs,

and salmon swimming upstream.
Just before we die we will
hear it too, turning like a key. No matter

who calls to us we won't return, the cold river
beyond our dreams suddenly important.
The children of Hamelin heard the music

and they had no need for wagons or blankets,
no need for the years that once stretched
ahead of them; their parents, stunned,

will never stop listening.

My Grandfather's Last Errand

He rose from his chair in the living room
and walked down the hall, pausing

in the kitchen where evening had begun
to pour through the windows as water

must have poured into the Titanic.
He believed he was running

an errand so he did not hug
my grandmother, who spoke to him

from the study, and he did not linger,
admiring his life's furniture. He would

never again turn the knob on his front door,
wouldn't open his bed that night, or look out

at his trees sinking into winter's
deep blue. He was leaving on his last errand

and, on the way, he passed the cemetery
where his parents waited for him, under

years of earth, passed the houses where
he once knew every neighbor's name,

the post office where he sorted letters,
the cabin where he spent summers

watching a river sing. Even as I tell this
the rooms where I loved him are disappearing:

the piano wet and heavy, the tables
where we sat together floating away.

The Dog Watched Television

The summer of my mother's illness,
a season so hot and dry it might
have erupted in flames, we discovered
the dog liked television. She barked
if we left her alone in the dim silence
of the bedroom but was cheerful
if we provided a documentary
about whales. She learned why
prehistoric wolves were likely to
care for their sick and injured while
we drove my mother, fasting,
to the operating room and kicked
the broken dishwasher and forgot
garbage day for so many weeks
the utility room became an odor.
The dog watched Billy the Exterminator
capture raccoons and alligators
and restore them to their natural habitats;
she watched *The Civil War*, learned
about our national parks, considered
the troubles facing our oceans.
My mother wept and raged and drank
clear liquids and worried that none of us
loved her enough, and the dog settled
her narrow head on a pillow,
her black eyes wise.

Amelia Earhart's First Flight

She was tall and pretty so she caught the eye
of a pilot at the fair and he drove his plane
towards her while she stood still, unafraid

of being hit, felt the power of his wings lifting.
This is how it began: a stranger
picking her out of a crowd, a ten minute flight
on which she saw how small her life was:

her house the size of a radio,
the trees she spent her childhood climbing
no larger than her hands, the rules
she intended to break too tiny to matter.

Hamelin Without the Rats

It was gone: the sound of chewing in the darkness,
the trail of feet through flour
on the kitchen floor. You could not hear them

gathering in the walls, did not
find them eating in the alleys behind restaurants:
standing on their hind legs,

their nude tails pale in the moonlight.
Hamelin without the rats was a place
without shadows or malice: food waited

unattended on tables and babies
slept on blankets on the floor. Everything
was vulnerable, quiet, unguarded.

Doors stood open, and women walked
alone at night, and children played
in the cemeteries, unafraid of ghosts.

It was safe to be naked, to tell the truth,
to open the windows so the neighbors
could see. Shopkeepers did not hide

their money and they did not watch for thieves.
Hamelin without the rats was so quiet
people could hear the river, even when

they were sleeping, and the mountains
gathered darkly in their windows:
purple and blue, each dawn, like a bruise.

The Silk Road

The first time I read about the Black Death
in some middle school social studies class
I was afraid. It followed the Silk Road,
our teacher said, moved from one
port town to another on the backs of rats.
I had already imagined camels and spices,
the way fabric became more valuable
each time it was sold. But I had not
thought of diseases moving through
the mountains and deserts, had not
yet seen the drawings of people dressed
in bird masks, or whipping themselves
for their sins. We went back to reading
about pepper and ginger, about desert sands
that shifted so quickly whole cities were buried
and caravans disappeared. But I lingered
over the paragraphs about people
sealed into their houses in a
primitive quarantine, the fires, the bodies
rotting in the streets. I found a passage
about how thieves went into the rooms
of the dead and helped themselves
to jewels and feasts, slept
in dangerous, elegant beds.
Silk, we read, was made first by worms
and suddenly all those roads to the past
squirmed with them: spinning and devouring,
glowing, opening little spaces in the earth.

My Brother, Trying To Go Home

It was evening when my brother stood at the window
with a sleeping bag and flashlight, and we watched

him walking down the narrow street, towards the empty house
we had not yet sold. He moved through the high grass,

past the sign that meant it would soon belong
to someone else, and entered the darkness

of our abandoned life. Sometimes I see him
standing in the place where the stairs turn

towards the bedroom he did not want to leave.
He slept on the floor, for weeks, while the rest

of us were elsewhere: hanging pictures on walls,
standing in new closets, arranging

the furniture of the future.

Orpheus Singing in the Underworld

He went to the end of the world searching
for an entrance and, when he found one,
grief filled him with music. His voice moved

huge stones and opened iron gates
and caused Cerberus to lay down
his three heads. He sang about how much

he missed Euridyce and how badly
he wanted her back; his music caused
the fluttering shades to hush; the Erinyes

dropped their whips and wept tears
of blood. The underworld was dark
and still and Persephone, on her black

marble throne, began to weep.
She knew what it meant to be stolen
while you were young; she knew

how snakes and chariots moved
beneath golden meadows.
Each ghost remembered someone

they loved but could not touch.
In the underworld's garden,
whispering poplars and weeping willows

felt the absence of birds in their branches.

Titanic Survivors Found Onboard

after the headline in the Weekly World News

They had been down there for decades, waiting.
The women wore billowing dresses and the men,
unable to smoke their cigars, or read their wet
newspapers, stood on the submerged deck

with their hands in their pockets. These were
the people who had not found a place on the lifeboats,
the ones who heard every song the band played.
Still, they did not drown or die of hypothermia but found

themselves living in those gorgeous, sunken rooms;
they drank tea from china cups and drifted
from deck to deck in a party of bubbles and fish.
The divers who found them were dazzled

by their happiness: the way they had managed
a sunken life. Once they had the chance,
these survivors weren't sure they wanted to leave.
Perhaps the Titanic needed them; its dance halls

and verandas shivered with memories
and, anyway, who knew if they could still stand
on dry land? They showed their visitors
how they tied themselves to their beds

at night, so they would not drift,
showed them the cavernous kitchen
where they had been helping themselves
to years of dessert. In the end, they stayed under the crush

of history, their watches stopped, stayed
with the sharks and whales, preferred the darkness,
the wreckage itself which understood them:
the way they had walked aboard with
trunks and tickets, but would never arrive
at their intended destination.

At Twelve

after the photos by Sally Mann

One girl sits on her father's lap at a dinner party,
her head turned towards the camera. Her hair
is tied with a ribbon and a season of flowers

blooms on her dress. This is a garden party
and the adults are deep in a conversation
she does not yet join. One girl, flung across

a white chair, has just emerged from a river.
A summer evening deepens around her
and the water glows with the remains

of childhood. My favorite, though, is a girl
who has outgrown her playhouse. She stands
on the porch like Alice after a drink of cordial

and the table where she once served tea
has shrunk and the doorway where she waits
will allow her to pass for one more year.

A man's arm reaches from the shadows
and it is impossible to say whether it belongs
to her father or a man she will someday love.

The arm might be protective or it might be
strangling; at any rate, the girl stands
on the brink of something, and we cannot tell

whether she is coming or going.

Ferry Ride to Ocracoke

My parents drove the great weight of their car
onto a barge that smelled of fuel and wind;

there must have been fifty families on each ship,
crossing the shallows between islands.

Evenings, we left a trail in the water
that seemed to lead to the moon. Each vessel

had its own seagulls that landed
on verandas, or flapped behind our progress,

and they were the color of heaven.
We leaned against railings

until the creatures of the deep
showed themselves to us: dolphins

slick with delight, whales sighing
for a moment before their descent.

In memory, I climb the staircase
to the place where I hold bread in my hand,

waiting for it to be taken; other times
I am watching docks and cottages remember

themselves after a fog, listening to our low horn
ask its one question.

Sight

Go north a dozen years
on a road overgrown with vines
to find the days after you were born.
Flowers remembered their colors and trees
were frothy and the hospital was

behind us now, its brick indifference
forgotten by our car mirrors. You were
revealed to me: tiny, delicate,
your head smelling of some other world.
Turn right after the circular room

where I kept my books and right again
past the crib where you did not sleep
and you will find the window where
I held you that June morning
when you opened your eyes. They were

blue, tentative, not the deep chocolate
they would later become. You were gazing
into the world: at our walls,
my red cup, my sleepless hair and though
I'm told you could not focus, and you

no longer remember, we were seeing
one another after seasons of darkness.

This Fawn in Our Meadow

This fawn in our meadow is tucked among wildflowers
where she sleeps and nibbles her fur, lifts her nose

sometimes to sniff the wind. We watch her ears twitching
in the high grass, admire the way she stays

where she is placed, waiting hours for her mother
to come home. We are glad that our meadow contains

a cradle and that in it, each day, the fawn is able
to dream of fields and forests, safe from wolves

and lions, foxes and fast cars. You should see
her dappled back and sudden legs, her face

which has not known grief. She does not worry
about her mother crossing our street to find the river,

does not know about winter or hunting season.
Hidden in the deep leaves of summer, she must

imagine the grass is always this tall.

The Dead Take Vacations

Being dead is more exhausting than you might think
and the dead go sometimes to the resorts
they couldn't afford when they were alive.

Oh, the dead are sunning themselves
on all the world's beaches and, eating nothing,
they reserve empty tables by the sea.

They are dancing on verandas
in European hotels, listening to the blues,
smelling coffees and breads, floating

down the white slopes of ski mountains.
The dead can't go home so sometimes
these vacations last years. They meet

a dead friend on a sidewalk and spend a day
following a pair of strangers
through museums. They occupy unpopular

hotel rooms and enjoy the cold indifference
of the sheets. The dead are not on vacation
from a dull job or a disapproving

mother-in-law; they are trying to forget,
to distance themselves from
all the ways they were once vain

and unkind. The dead send post cards
to their dead relatives, leave them
in the curtains of cottages

that are closed for the season;
they have pictures of the past
and can travel

without stamps, and, on them,
the dead write nothing visible,
nothing we would understand.

Possum in the Garbage

He was a surprise of white: his teeth
like knives, his face a triangle
of albino dislike. I had seen him before,

on our back porch, where my father
sometimes left watermelon rinds,
and he dipped his tongue into them,

his skin glowing beneath our lights,
like some four-legged relative
of the moon. I knew him
as a citizen of the night:

a fainting, ghostly presence
with a tail so naked it was
embarrassed to drag behind him.

But that morning, terrified and violent,
he was different: a hissing fury
at the bottom of the garbage can,
a vampire bathed in light.

Algebra

There was an old woman my mother hired to tutor me
in Algebra and I remember the weight of the textbook
I carried that summer, the roads that wandered past lagoons

and mansions to a porch where my boredom increased.
I knew that I should not add apples and oranges,
that whatever I did to one side of an equation I must

do to the other. But everything else was mysterious
and vague: I wasn't interested in math, didn't want
to solve problems that already had solutions;
I didn't think there should be an order of operations

unless it was this: me going to the beach,
then reading novels with sex scenes,
then writing letters to my friends. I took
my homework to the pool where I left it

in a lounge chair, growing paler in the sun,
or I abandoned it on the lawn, near the failed garden
and lopsided mailbox, under a tree that had
grown short and crooked, balanced against the wind.

Polio Summer

Because it often struck in summer, the wealthy families
went away to mountain resorts, hoping the fresh air

might spare their children. My parents saw
suitcases and trunks each June, stacked beneath

the deep Magnolia trees. Movie theaters closed
and the velvet curtains inside filled with dust;

posters curled and faded in their glass
display cases; popcorn machines filled with

window light and silence. All the ordinary summer fun
stood empty: the carnivals where the carousels

and ferris wheels traced lonely circles, the blue pools
where a single child might dive, the beaches

where chairs were arranged on abandoned verandas:
seagulls flapping, the ocean itself white with fear.

Winter Arrives

Winter arrives like a box of knives.
Even now, my father's car spins off the road,
his tires blind and uncertain. These are

our first blizzards on North Mountain:
our meadow a sudden museum,
all trees like statues. I am not prepared

for the things I will lose in this season
of hospitals, each drafty corridor
made of ice. All night darkness expands

in our curtains; I wake to bad news:
a flapping of birds without wings.
One day I wear so many coats I cannot

be found; the future swallows
our hope and now a radio speaks
in warnings: its predictions

in inches, in feet.

Astronauts

Each time I try to imagine my grandfather's death
I watch him start the engine of his red truck
for a final drive, but I cannot allow him

to arrive in the place where he will die:
in a grocery store where he will wait
in line, his cart half full. I can't watch him

order the sliced ham, or fall down
holding it, can't find the faces of the people
nearby. He was 45 when I was born

and I was 45 when he died; I have
the notes and telegrams he received
the day I was born: each stamped

with a man walking on the moon.
He built me a bedroom at the top
of his stairs, painted blue, so I had my own

summer sky. First, I was the astronaut
arriving from the planet of my parents' affections,
unable to speak or walk. Then, he was

the astronaut: counting down on a starless
winter night, unexpectedly weightless.

Directions to Your College Dorm

All hallways still lead to that room
with its ceiling so high it might have been

a sky, and your metal bed by the window,
and your crate of books. First,

you must walk across the deep
winter campus to find your friend

throwing snowballs that float
for years. Then, open our letters:

shelves of words. You will find
our coats, our awkwardness, the tickets

from the trains that witnessed
our confusion. Love was the place

where we became as naked
as morning; it was dangerous and

dappled and we visited its shores
with suitcases and maps from childhood.

I remember our shadows growing
on your wall while a candle

swallowed itself. You kept a single
glass of water on a desk and it trembled

whenever we danced.

Quarantine, 1918

There were towns
that knew about the flu before
it arrived; they had time to imagine the germs
on a stranger's skirts, to see how death
could be sealed in an envelope,
how a fever could bloom in the evening,
and take a life overnight.
A few villages, deep in the mountains,
posted guards on their roads,
and no one was allowed to come or go,
not even a grandmother carrying a cake;
no mail was accepted and all the words
and packages families sent
to one another went unopened,
unanswered. Trains were told
not to stop, so they glowed for a moment
before swaying
towards some other place. The food
at the corner store never came
from out of town and no one went
to see a distant auntie
or state fair. For awhile, the outside world
existed in imagination, in memory,
in books or suitcases, deep in closets.
There was nothing but the town itself,
hiding from what was possible,
and the children cutting dolls
from paper, their scissors sharp.

Fishing Pier

There was a fishing pier, in childhood,
attached to a restaurant, where my father
took me to eat grilled cheese sandwiches
on Saturdays. Standing up
in my booth, I pressed my nose
to the window which framed
a sleepless sea. The pier was crooked
and stood on bird legs; hurricanes
made it drunk. When we walked
on it I could see through the spaces
between the boards where the writhing
was deep. All around us fishermen
cast their lines into the hunger;

sometimes they braced themselves
against the nudity of a fish,
pulled from the currents
no one can explain. It was here
that I learned about magnetism
and migrations, about the influence
of the moon. I would return
to this pier all my life: blown home
by high winds; I sat under it
with my grandfather, my daughter,
my dog. The color of the sea
is unreliable and I watched it
change: calm blue, evening black,
stormy white like a rabid animal's mouth.
I filled my buckets with sizzling water,
buried myself in sand.

The Weather in Hamelin

The weather in Hamelin was often mild:
a mist over the countryside in morning, from which

cottages and villagers emerged. It was
warm enough in summer that children

swam in the river, then gathered
in the branches of apple trees, their faces

as bright as fruit. In winter, their sleds
left trails on the far hills and you could hear

them screaming as they slid into the shadow
of the valley. In spring, they climbed

the mountain itself, though it took all day,
and brought picnics in baskets:

sausages and hard bread, cider and cheese.
They spread out on flat rocks and the girls

wore dresses as soft as water
while boys hid beneath

the brims of their hats.
In fall they favored their

red coats, and walked to school on a road
slick with dying leaves. For awhile,

color clung to the trees, then it was only
on the ground, then the first frost made

the windows of their houses into jewels,
and the earth stiffened.

Dunes, At Night

They are white by day, arranged by the wind,
with their glittering grasses and low peasant trees.
But by evening they are blue with shadows
and their valleys are cold and soft.

They have listened to whispers and hisses
and wolves: the endless beating of the sea.
By night they are gray, as if drawn in pencil,
or black if the moon is veiled. You can carry

a lantern and follow them the way you might
follow a map made of breath; they know
the sorrow of the stars and they remember,
for awhile, the feet that have passed
over them on the way to daydreams or boats.

My Mother, Eating Chocolate

She kept a package of chocolate almonds
in the car, ate them while she waited at stoplights.

She bought brownies -- dark, forbidden --
and hid them in the refrigerator, behind the eggs

and milk. She stirred chocolate into her coffee,
baked it into cakes she would slice, late at night,

in her pajamas, after the rest of us went to bed.
When she was nervous, or had received bad news,

she found a piece of chocolate and sat down
to unwrap it, each bite like a ripening fire.

There was chocolate in her desk drawers
and chocolate in her purse; her hair

was the color of chocolate and she liked mahogany
furniture, dark hallways with portraits hung

in heavy frames. She liked night more than day:
the world sunk in chocolate, our trees wet with it,

the river behind our house melting into the stars.

Desert

The desert was barren and what grew there
was made of thorns and stone. I could tell you
how we drifted into the deep blue relief
of sleep, how we stepped barefoot

into that morning's canyon. Each Joshua Tree
and cactus was a study in thirst, in strangled
emotion. The desert was a place beyond
weeping and I could have stayed there forever,

feeling nothing, while the coyote wandered
under the clean map of night.

He Was About to Come Home

It seemed to me that he was about to come home.
The walls thought of him and grew taller. His blue chair,
in the corner by the bookshelf, expected him

to settle again into the afternoon's reading.
His bed waited for the weight of him, descending
into sleep, and his bath robe hung, wilted,

from a closet door. He would come back to us
because his favorite foods were still
in the cupboards, and his toothbrush was damp

on the sink, and his jug of milk had not yet expired.
He would come back in the darkness,
when we had given up, each of us thin

with despair. I imagined the motor
of his red truck in the driveway, the sound
of his feet in the hall. It seemed to me

that he was about to come home, that we could
bring him back from the land of the dead if we had
the right desire, if we could slip into the shadows

of pomegranates and weeping willows
and sing like Orpheus. He was about to come home
and explain the mistake: how the doctors were

wrong, how death passed like a fever,
and we would make his tea with sugar
and the house itself would be relieved:

each curtain alive with wind, each lamp a flower.

My Father, Eating

He liked banging on crabs with a hammer,
the meat white and shy, or cracking

the shells of sunflower seeds with his teeth.
Oysters pleased him because they hid

in thick, ugly mouths like tongues.
While working on briefs or arguments

he opened pistachio nuts, one after
another, their shells falling around him

on the floor: cradles for ladybugs,
beige cups of nothing. He preferred

fish with a million hidden bones,
each one impossible to remove,

veined shrimp, lobsters
opened with tools that belonged

in a hospital. Even hungry, he enjoyed
working, liked an orange more than

an apple, a pomegranate
more than a banana: that underworld

of seeds beneath the skin.

Tire Swing

It hung in front of a farmhouse,
from the branches of late summer,

and when I held onto the rope
I was inside the color green

which was as deep and cool
as water. The tire itself

knew my grandfather's fields,
had driven through his rows

of longing: all corn ripening
in silk. Sometimes I faced

a porch where a screen door
slapped against departure and

a cat's tail traced
the memory of light.

Angry Fathers

When I was a child the mothers were sad and trapped,
weeping into the monotony of their laundry,
stifled by the world's ideas, which were as dreary
as housework. But the fathers were angry --

so mad even the furniture grew worried
when they came home from work: the chairs
and lamps cautious, the dishes unsteady.
My friends had fathers so frightening

we hid when they pulled into the driveway,
their engines roaring like lions;
we ran away to the woods where
it was safe to laugh. These fathers

had swollen faces and abdomens
that would not fit into their pants; they talked
about reality and hard work and how much
things cost. They sat at their wobbly

kitchen tables where their wives
served anemic meats and coffee
so strong they would never
find sleep. They looked overgrown

to me, these men, as if their forks
were too small and their couches
were too floral, too dainty. One of them
screamed so loudly I dropped

my water glass: shards around me like fear.
The mothers had pinched mouths
and worry lines and nervous habits
but the fathers were dangerous like Pompeii;

they had the manners of a volcano;
their moods hung over us like ash.

Dog Guarding a House in Pompeii

Surely he had a bark
he used to defend his perimeter,

a name, a bone he carried
into the next life. There was a hole

he never stopped digging, a child
he preferred to sleep beside,

a column he sniffed before lifting
his leg. Here he is, cast in ash,

still guarding the past, having
worried for days in the atrium

over changes in the sky.
Someone should come home

to him, he has been loyal
all these years; even his tail

remembers.

Grendel's Mother

You can imagine how she felt when she found her son's hand.
She wanted something more than revenge.
Don't most wars begin and end in grief?
It makes no difference who lives in the castle and who lives in the swamp.
Anyone can be a monster.
The truth is on fire.

Only an ocean is as beautiful and dangerous as fire.
There are maps in every hand.
The things we fear become monsters.
Love is as ancient as revenge.
Grendel's mother knew each chamber of their swamp.
She had seen Cain wet with grief.

Cain was thin with neglect, chilled by grief.
He trembled, even beside a fire.
East of Eden, he found this swamp.
Sometimes he stared into the mystery of his own hand.
Had he been ruined by revenge?
Was he a monster?

The people of the village called Grendel a monster.
It is true: his appetites caused them grief.
They spent years plotting revenge:
saw his shape move through their fires,
knew he could rip them apart with his huge hands.
His origins were as murky as his swamp.

It is difficult to navigate in a swamp.
Something hungry lurks beneath the surface;
death might reach for you like a hand.
Trees hang low over the waters of grief.
Light a fire;
plan your revenge.

After all, the world begins and ends with stories of revenge.
It is always night in the swamp.
Each sword is forged in fire.
Only you know the name of your monster.
Only you know the depths of your grief.
There is strength in your hand.

Grendel's mother was a monster.
She knew the shape of grief.
She held her son's hand.

Chasing Fireflies

We stood on childhood's lawn in evening, and our front porches
were islands, and the deep shadowed grass was a sea.
We carried the glass jars our mothers plucked from

their cupboards and we were chasing fireflies.
If you had painted us in blue and black beneath a cup
of stars it would have been difficult to know for certain

what we caught, hard to say what glowed for a moment
and what darkened and slipped away. It was just
a week in July when we were called from our hammocks

by the velvet light of desire, our jars open like mouths.

The Fejee Mermaid

A baboon head was sewn to an orangutan torso
which was attached to a salmon's tail. She lived

in museums and halls: one hand pressed to her face,
the other limp at her side. Her mouth was opened

in surprise or horror, her teeth sharp.
P.T. Barnum said she was found by a fisherman

and bought by an English gentleman and
the crowds were astonished by her ugliness

for they had been dreaming of the mermaids
in picture books with their bare breasts

and long hair. She went to South Carolina
where two newspapers fought over her pedigree,

to museums in Boston and New York,
to London where she enjoyed the gaze

of Duchesses in hats. Who knows how she felt,
displaying herself like that: out of water,

her story invented by a man who sold lies.
She may or may not have been ruined by fire,

the facts of her exit as soft as smoke.

The Owl

She was no larger than my hand and I met her at night,
the beam of my headlights bringing noon
to the branch she preferred. She did not fly away

but stood in my unexpected sun, her eyes
surrounded by white feathers and wind,
and she was gorgeous, interrupted in her underworld

of ghosts and mice as Persephone must have been
each spring when she was asked to leave behind
her forgetful river and weeping willows

and stand in the glare of her mother's love.

Bermuda Triangle

For instance the U.S.S. *Cyclops* which disappeared without
a distress call and left no wreckage, or the
World War II bombers that vanished somewhere
between Miami and Bermuda. Beneath these waters,

was the lost continent of Atlantis; in the sky:
a large, glowing sphere that pulsated from yellow
to orange. Before radio contact was lost,
one aircraft sent this message:

Everything looks strange, even the ocean. We are
entering white water. My science books suggested
rogue waves, one hundred feet high, tropical cyclones,
methane hydrates. But I knew

from my father's lost comb in the bathroom
or the way I always had one sock, not two,
or the way my cat walked beneath our house
one day and never came out, no matter

how I called for her, that there were certain
disappearances that were unexplained,
certain lights no one would ever identify, certain
triangles where time and direction changed

and, inside these, you couldn't send a distress signal
to your old life, could not be located
by search parties or naval planes.

Early Hominids Slept In Trees

This was before they slipped into caves
and painted the drama of the hunt, before
their stone tools and splendid fires,
when early hominids filled the trees
like night. They climbed a ladder
of branches into evening where they
arranged themselves beneath
the applause of leaves. There were
wind storms and lightning and somehow
babies were held and people snored
or turned over. Surely someone was
afraid of heights? And someone
must have secured a place at the bottom,
or slept on the ground, demonstrating
how it might be done? Balanced up there,
in the mythic beginning, they were
safer from predators that walked
on four legs, swishing tails.
They clung to the trunk: felt the world
growing colder, the new power in their thumbs.
Trees were like houses and going home
meant climbing into the sky where words
appeared inside them like stars.

How Dinosaurs Died

Some were as large as city buildings
and some were the size of chickens.
I have read, of course, the asteroid theory:
collision, dust, ruined sunlight.
For millions of years they grew their
scales and tails, stood on
hind legs with hollow bones.
There is the theory of volcanic activity:
hot lava and ash, some unbreathable night.

No one knows for sure how it happened:
ice age, shifting continents,
quick and vicious plague? Dinosaurs
worried the seas and skies, tended eggs,
nibbled the shade from trees,
until, at last, they did not. I am told our birds
are their descendants: flapping in patterns,
migrating, rising all at once
from fields in evening, fishing
on the beaches of my childhood,
taking bread from my hand.

Lover's Eyes

They were sent during courtship in lockets and boxes:
tiny ivory portraits of the eye. This gaze

arrived like a letter and could be opened
or closed. Alone and framed

the eye awaited moments when
the beloved might watch it glisten like a fish

in its aquarium of affection. Each was private
and blind: a pupil opening in a room

it could not admire. This was a time of grief rings
and hair wreaths, when people held onto

fragments and pieces, a time when
desire was beneath heavy lashes,

unblinking.

Missing My Grandfather

He isn't coming back, yet I wait for him:
in his chair by the window, in the meadow
where we once flew a kite. I wait for him

under the breathless tree which widens
each year outside his farmhouse,
beside a photograph in which we stand

together in that distant summer,
squinting into the white future. I wait for him
in all the seasons where he has gone

missing: the one in which I float
down a river made of time, the one
in which I build nothing from snow.

I wait for him under the pier where
we once played cards, and in the truck
where his maps knew the highways

that spilled off the page: the ones
that did not end.

My Mother, Running Away From Home

She is tiny and defiant and she has
packed her suitcase with marbles, is running

along the dirt road at the edge of the family farm.
Later, a cousin or uncle will find her

a mile away in a field of corn which grows
green and tall: each ear listening to silk.

My grandfather says she did it a dozen times
in childhood: packed nothing useful

and ran on bare feet, her hair tangled.
I liked this story, asked to hear it at holidays

where someone was always willing to tell me
how she let the screen door slam,

before running towards a place she could not quite
find, running the way deer run

when they are frightened, or cats:
their legs seeming to multiply.

Mailing Babies

For a few years it was legal to mail children
under fifty pounds and parents bought stamps
and I do not know if babies wore them

on their foreheads. Men with heavy mailbags
delivered kids to their grandmothers
or aunties, carried them over rural routes

which passed through forests and farmlands,
to front porches and someone hanging
laundry against the sky. One baby,

in Maryland, never woke to notice her trip.
A girl named Edna was sent from Virginia
to Florida for fifteen cents. Parents went

to the post office and mailed their children
who were delivered amid packages
and envelopes: weighed and addressed

and handed to men who also carried
fish and chickens, cats and bricks.
I like thinking of the babies, traveling

from one farmhouse to another:
fragile, handled with care, their feet
tucked into a mail bag,

dirt roads passing slowly below.

Picking Apples With My Father

This was October, when the world burns,
and we found ourselves in an orchard, climbing trees.

We had not lived a full year on the mountain so we had
not seen our apple trees in spring, burdened

with blossoms, and we had not seen them in winter:
hunched and starved, growing old beneath

the stars. My father had never fallen, his car
was uncrushed by the side of the road. Any apple

my daughter wanted, he would help her reach.
I remember how he put her on his shoulders

or moved himself from limb to limb, picking.
We wanted more than we could eat.

Visiting Emily's House

Alive, I might have found her in the garden
or walking in the hills beside her dog. Instead,
her white dress hung at the top of the stairs,

in front of a window, where she once watched
the circus redden; it was lost,
without her. Next, her bedroom door

hung open, revealing floorboards
and leafy light. Downstairs, her piano stood stiffly,
waiting for music,

its keys like bones. In letters she is
carrying baskets and notes, opening gates,
bent over her rising bread.

I came looking for her but found instead
her lanterns, her myopic windows,
her cooking pans and foot paths; I stood

in the rooms of her life,
admiring her view.

My Mother, Dreaming of Privacy

Other mothers dreamed of Hawaiian vacations or expensive furniture;
they wanted to be noticed in their evening dresses,
to be liked by the neighbors, but my mother dreamed

of privacy. When she said the word she might have
been biting into a late summer peach. She loved distances,
and messages in bottles, lost forever at sea. She liked vines

and attics, and doors, buried treasure, hidden keys.
She closed the shutters, pulled the drapes, untied
the curtains and let them fall. She hated

bikinis and questions but enjoyed candles in winter,
wore coats with hidden pockets. She danced by herself,
and sketched alone, her pencil quiet; she liked hats,

and wigs, and sunglasses, possums pretending to sleep.

Weather

There is weather on the day you are born
and weather on the day you die. There is
the year of drought, and the year of floods,
when everything rises and swells,
the year when winter will not stop falling,
and the year when summer lightning
burns the prairie, makes it disappear.
There are the weathervanes, dizzy
on top of farmhouses, hurricanes
curled like cats on a map of sky;
there are cows under the trees outlined
in flies. There is the weather that blows
a stranger into town, and the weather
that changes suddenly: an argument,
a sickness, a baby born
too soon. Crops fail and a field becomes
a study in hunger; storm clouds
billow over the sea;
tornadoes appear like the drunk
trunks of elephants. People talking about
weather are people who don't know what to say
and yet the weather is what happens to all of us:
the blizzard that makes our neighborhoods
strange, the flood that carries away
our plans. We are getting ready for the weather,
or cleaning up after the weather, or enduring
the weather. We are drenched in rain
or sweat; we are looking for an umbrella,
a second mitten; we are gathering
wood to build a fire.

My Life in a Picasso Painting

Sometimes I have five eyes, sometimes two noses.
I am oppressed by angles or moods, by years

when I find myself dressed in blue. First,
I strum a guitar: my head fallen,

my hand like a claw. Then, I am naked,
bathing myself in milk, while the bed

behind me whitens. It is my back you study,
my bones that arrange themselves

in triangular patterns. If I kiss you,
everything in the room will brighten.

If I dream, a river will run between my legs.
My feet have vanished, waiting for you

to come home.

Jellyfish

Fabric hearts, fancy mushrooms,
ribbons of stings, a pulsing

desire to colonize the warm places
in the sea. They are ghostly umbrellas,

memories of buttons, drifting
colors of ruffled impulse.

They glow the way a place
glows when it cannot be reached

anymore because it parachutes
in time.

The Land Of Nod

It was East of Eden in a valley made of jealousy and regret.
Cain was the first child to find he was not the favorite,
that his father preferred another. Maybe he built
a sharp stone shack where he was never warm
or maybe he slept in a cave. I think Cain could smell

Eden blooming, its fruits sweet and luminous,
and I think, sometimes, a warm breeze blew to him
from that other life. He was tossed out because
he could not control his disappointment
and rage, because he wished, for a moment,

that he had no brother. Now his failings
hung loosely from him like the clothes he fashioned
from clouds; now he considered, again and again,
how he might have done it all differently. Sometimes
the ghost of Abel appeared to him in the fires he lit

to keep himself company: his brother, whom he
could not love, restless and flickering among the flames.

Our House, Surrounded by Animals

They came up the driveway, through the meadow,
over the ridge, into the forest, the valley, the sky.
There was a bear with a body made of night,
a snake so endless it might have been a river,
a lone turkey who wandered on stick legs,
his blue chin wagging. We found deer sleeping
in front of our doors, the grass crushed
by their dreams; there was a woodpecker
with a sharp head, a mountain lion that became
a tail and a set of tracks. We lived inside the migrations
of birds, our windows blackened with patterns.
We were surrounded by animals and weather:
high winds, lightning that reminded me of veins,
snow so deep we brought our groceries home
by sled. Our house was made of hunting
and hiding, of hooves, and claws, and wings.

Addresses

There was the house my cousin and I built as children --
circular, stacked, made from a pile of white brick;
we pretended it had a number, painted it
on the side. But no address for the tree
I wanted to occupy for years: all light altered

by my position in the canopy. No mailbox
at that shack in the sand where we spent two weeks
with a weasel and a lantern and a pillow
made of ocean. We slept in a tent that turned
the world blue, in a field stitched with stars,

on a porch, under a sand blanket beneath a pier.
Our first home was a cottage and our second
was so vast even the cat was lost.
White envelopes that knew our names
could not find us. Who knows what they meant to bring?

No address when I am dead and, in the meantime,
I will occupy my daughter's treehouse:
North Mountain, Lost River, to the right
of the spider webs and binoculars,
just beyond the ghost of the dog of childhood.

Portsmouth Island

Drive across two islands and ride a ferry
to find the quiet. There are gulls flapping against
the blue rules of the sky, Pelicans with beaks
drawn by some ancient cartoonist. You must find

a fisherman with room for you in his carved boat,
beside the nets and pots, near the place
where life has gills. There is an island beyond
the other islands, beyond the moment when
the current insists, where you can walk through

an abandoned village, sit on a front porch
among striped cats. Here, the shells have grown pink
and the wind has grown wise and the last inhabitant
packed a bag many years ago for some other shore.
You can find your own home among the clams

and mosquitoes, among the gravestones
that have lost their dates and names to hurricanes.
Step into the trees and you will see your grandmother
rebuilding the past with sand: her dress wet,
her hair as gray as a gathering storm.

Meet Me In Hamelin

Meet me in Hamelin, before the children heard the music,
before the rats drowned themselves in history,
before the Piper himself: dressed in red, carrying

that magic pipe. Meet me near the church where
the stained glass window is not yet hung, beside
Wesser river -- breathless, rushing -- where we'll climb

the winding path to Kloppenburg Hill. Beyond this:
forests, and beyond these, dancing: the kind
we haven't tried since we were young; place one

hand on my shoulder, one hand on my back,
while the wind moves like water through the branches
of night. Meet me before the mayor refuses to pay,

before the day when only three girls are left behind:
one too lame to run, one too deaf to hear,
one blind and unable to follow. They have been

waiting for us in all the versions of the story:
in the caves and rivers, in the handsome land
where the Piper managed his revenge. Meet me

in Hamelin before all that, hold my hand,
walk with me through the unswept streets,
where the children are unharmed.

About the Author

(author photography by Gordon Kreplin)

Biography

Faith Shearin is the author of four previous books of poetry: *The Owl Question* (May Swenson Award), *The Empty House* (Word Press), *Moving the Piano*, and *Telling the Bees* (SFA University Press). Recent work has appeared in *Alaska Quarterly Review* and *Poetry East* and has been read aloud by Garrison Keillor on *The Writer's Almanac*. She is the recipient of awards from The Fine Arts Work Center in Provincetown, The Barbara Deming Memorial Fund, and the National Endowment for the Arts. Her work also appears in The Autumn House Anthology of Contemporary Poets and in Good Poems, American Places. She lives with her husband, her daughter, a tarantula, and two dogs, in a cabin on top of a mountain in West Virginia.

Dogfish Head Craft Brewed Ales

Dogfish Head is the first American craft brewery to focus on culinary-inspired beer recipes outside traditional beer styles and it has done so since the day it opened with the motto "off-centered ales for off-centered people." Since 1995, Dogfish has redefined craft beer and the way people think about beer by brewing with unique ingredients.

Today, Dogfish is among the fastest-growing breweries in the country and has won numerous awards throughout the years. Dogfish Head has grown into a 200+ person company with a restaurant/brewery/distillery in Rehoboth Beach, a beer-themed inn on the harbor in Lewes and a production brewery/distillery in Milton, Delaware.

Dogfish Head currently sells beer in 31 states, and is proud to sponsor The Dogfish Head Poetry prize, awarded now for thirteen consecutive years!

Previous Winners of The Dogfish Head Poetry Prize

2014 Lucian Mattison, *Peregrine Nation*
The Broadkill River Press, Milton, Delaware

2013 Grant Clauser, *Necessary Myths*
The Broadkill River Press, Milton, Delaware

2012 Tina Raye Dayton, *The Softened Ground*
The Broadkill Press, Milton, DE

2011 Sherry Gage Chappelle, *Salmagundi*
The Broadkill Press, Milton, DE

2010 Amanda Newell, *Fractured Light*
The Broadkill Press, Milton, DE

2009 David P. Kozinski, *Loopholes*
The Broadkill Press, Milton, DE

2008 Linda Blaskey, *Farm*
Bay Oak Publishers, Dover, DE

2007 Anne Agnes Colwell,
Father's Occupation, Mother's Maiden Name
Bay Oak Publishers, Dover, DE

2006 Scott Whitaker, *Field Recordings*
Bay Oak Publishers, Dover, DE

2005 Michael Blaine, *Murmur*
Bay Oak Publishers, Dover, DE

2004 Emily Lloyd, *The Most Daring of Transplants*
Argonne House Press, Washington, DC

2003 James Keegan *Of Fathers and Sons*
Argonne House Press, Washington, DC

Other Titles from The Broadkill River Press

Sounding the Atlantic — Poetry by Martin Galvin
ISBN 978-0-9826030-1-7 — $14.95

That Deep & Steady Hum — Poetry by Mary Ann Larkin
ISBN 978-0-9826030-2-4 — $14.95

Exile at Sarzanna — Poetry by Laura Brylawski-Miller
ISBN 978-0-9826030-5-5 — $12.00

The Year of the Dog Throwers — Poetry by Sid Gold
ISBN 978-0-9826030-3-1 — $12.00

Domain of the Lower Air ‡ — Fiction by Maryanne Khan
ISBN 978-0-9826030-4-8 — $14.95

Speed Enforced by Aircraft *† — Poetry by Richard Peabody
ISBN 978-0-9826030-6-2 — $15.95

Dutiful Heart — Poetry by Joy Gaines-Friedler
ISBN 978-1-940120-91-1 — $16.00

Necessary Myths þ — Poetry by Grant Clauser
ISBN 978-1-940120-92-8 — $14.95

Postcard from Bologna ‡ — Poetry by Howard Gofreed
ISBN 978-1-940-120-90-4 — $15.95

Lemon Light — Poetry by H. A. Maxson
ISBN 978-1-940120-94-2 — $15.95

Peregrine Nation þ — Poetry by Lucian Mattison
ISBN 978-1-940120-85-0 — $15.95

On Gannon Street — Poetry by Mary Ann Larkin
ISBN 978-1-940120-86-7 — $12.00

The Table of the Elements * — Poetry by J. T. Whitehead
ISBN 978-1-940120-93-5 — $15.95

Good with Oranges * — Poetry by Sid Gold
ISBN 978-1-940120-83-6 — $16.00

(* NBA Nominees) († Pulitzer Prize Nominee)
(‡ NBCC Award nominee)(þ Dogfish Head Poetry Prize Winner)

CPSIA information can be obtained at www.ICGtesting.com
Printed in the USA
LVOW07s0405171115

462750LV00002B/2/P

9 781940 120973